DEC   2014   CR

A Great Idea
ENGINEERING

The Great Wall of China

By Don Nardo

NORWOOD HOUSE PRESS

Cover: The Great Wall winds its way over the mountain ranges of northern China.

Norwood House Press
P.O. Box 316598
Chicago, Illinois 60631

For information regarding Norwood House Press, please visit our Web site at:
www.norwoodhousepress.com or call 866-565-2900.

LIBRARY OF CONGRESS CATALOGING-IN-PUBLICATION DATA

Nardo, Don, 1947-
  The Great Wall of China / by Don Nardo.
    pages cm. -- (A great idea)
  Includes bibliographical references and index.
  Summary: "Describes the struggles and accomplishments in building the Great Wall of China. Includes glossary, websites, and bibliography for further reading"-- Provided by publisher.
  ISBN 978-1-59953-597-5 (library edition : alk. paper)
  ISBN 978-1-60357-590-4 (ebook)
  1. Great Wall of China (China)--Juvenile literature. I. Title.
  DS793.G67N37 2013
  931--dc23
                                                          2013011172

Manufactured in the United States of America in Stevens Point, Wisconsin.
254R—042014

Contents

Note: Words that are **bolded** in the text are defined in the glossary.

Chapter 1

Protection for the Middle Kingdom

It was just after dawn one morning in the early 1900s. A British woman named Mildred Cable was riding in a donkey cart. She was a Christian **missionary**. She wanted to bring Christianity to the Chinese. She had started to carry her message to some of China's small country villages. At the time, few Europeans, Americans, or other Westerners had ever visited that distant land.

Suddenly, Cable saw something remarkable up ahead. "Toward the west," she later wrote, was "the outline of a mighty fortress." Moving closer, she saw that this fort was part of a huge stone wall. Its dark outline stood out "against the morning sky." As the cart drew closer to the wall, she saw a towering stone watchtower. "From it," she wrote, "the long line of the wall dipped into a valley." Then

The Great Wall of China is the longest structure ever built by humans.

it "climbed a hill and vanished over its summit."

The wall Cable described is the largest structure ever built by humans. The Chinese call it **Chang Cheng**. Those words translate as "Great Wall" in English. More often than not, people refer to it as the Great Wall of China.

An Element of Mystery

Actually, calling it *the* Great Wall is a bit misleading. That is because this huge artifact is not a single structure. Rather, it is made of a long string of separate walls. Some were made of earth. Others were made of bricks and/or stone blocks.

The various pieces of the wall were built by several different Chinese rulers. Each added one or more new sections to those built by others. Building all of the wall's pieces took about 1,800 years. That is more than seven times longer than the United States has been a nation.

The Great Wall was built by a number of dynasties over the course of 1,800 years.

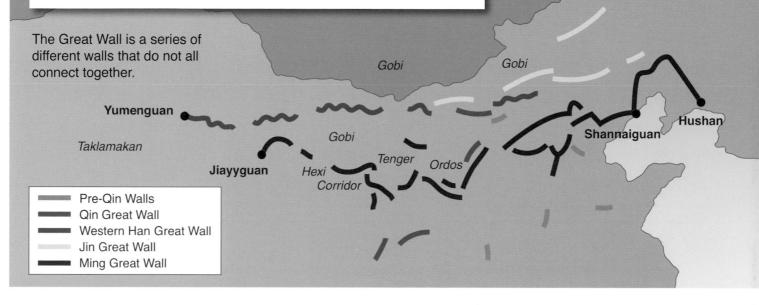

The Many Walls of the Great Wall

The Great Wall is a series of different walls that do not all connect together.

Gobi

Gobi

Yumenguan

Taklamakan

Gobi

Jiayyguan

Hexi Corridor

Tenger

Ordos

Shannaiguan

Hushan

Pre-Qin Walls
Qin Great Wall
Western Han Great Wall
Jin Great Wall
Ming Great Wall

The giant structure itself is very long. The exact length is not known. In fact, it may never be known. Part of the reason is that some sections have crumbled and vanished over the years. It is very hard for **archaeologists** and other experts to tell how long the missing sections were.

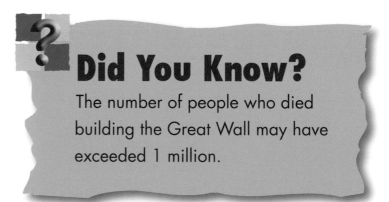

Did You Know?

The number of people who died building the Great Wall may have exceeded 1 million.

"As thousands of years pass, some ground structures disappear," Chinese official Yan Jianmin states. "We do not know where the walls used to be. When some local governments or companies develop the land, like coal mining or building new roads, they destroy the remaining parts under the ground."

Hidden parts of the wall are found from time to time. In 2012 Chinese **excavators** said they found several missing pieces of the wall.

Because of this, estimates for the wall's total length vary a lot. On the low side is 4,000 miles (6,400km). Other estimates range up to 6,200 miles (10,000km) or even more. (The bigger number is twice the width of the United States.)

China's Early Dynasties

Beginning around the 1600s BC, dynasties became common in China. A dynasty is a family line of rulers. Usually, when a dynastic king dies, his powers pass to his son. Or it might be a brother, nephew, or other relative. (In rarer cases the ruler's wife, mother, or daughter might take over as queen.) When the second king dies, another family member takes the throne, and so on. The earliest Chinese dynasty is believed to have been the Xia dynasty (about 2070–c.1600).

China's River Civilization

The Chinese had an important reason for building the wall. Two different cultures developed in the area. Close to 3,000 years ago, that area stretched across most of central and eastern Asia. Some of this huge area was well populated. A dense network of farms dotted the plains and valleys along the Yang-tse and Yellow Rivers. This river civilization was one of ancient China's two major cultures.

The rivers made that civilization possible. The soil in the region was very fertile. And the rivers supplied plenty of water for growing wheat, millet, and other crops. The farmers also raised pigs, sheep, and other animals. The crops the farmers grew supplied thousands of people

The Yang-tse River made ample farmland possible.

in the area. In addition to the dozens of larger towns and cities.

These towns and cities had a high level of culture. They created writings and paintings. They also developed music and philosophy. They had palaces, temples, and other large, beautiful buildings. The Chinese of this area called their region *Zhongguo*. The term means "Middle Kingdom." The name came from their belief that they lived at the center of the universe.

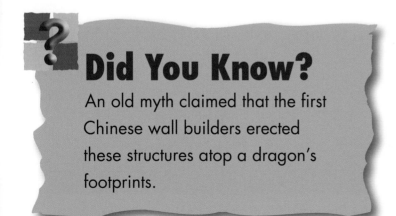

Did You Know?

An old myth claimed that the first Chinese wall builders erected these structures atop a dragon's footprints.

But for a long time, *Zhongguo*'s cities and districts were not united into a single nation. Up until the late 200s BC, most of the time they were divided into small, independent kingdoms. The rulers of these early Chinese kingdoms sometimes fought one another.

Peoples of the Steppes

As it turned out, these states had more to worry about than their quarrels. They also sometimes had to defend themselves from attacks. Beyond the Middle Kingdom stretched vast open plains and grasslands called **steppes**.

The steppes lay north and west of the river valleys. They were home to eastern Asia's other major ancient culture. It's people were mainly **nomads**. They

An Assault by Northern Nomads

One of the earliest known invasions of steppe nomads into China took place in the 800s BC. The rulers of the Zhou dynasty (about 1027 BC to 221 BC) sent soldiers to fight attackers from the north. These attackers were known as the Xianyun. A surviving poem quoted in Julia Lovell's 2006 book *The Great Wall: China Against the World, 1000 B.C.–A.D. 2000*, captures the Zhou war preparations. Part of it reads: "In the sixth month, all was bustle and excitement. The war chariots had been made ready." Another part states: "The Xianyun were in blazing force. There was no time to lose. The king had ordered the expedition to deliver the royal kingdom [from harm]."

had no permanent farms or settled towns. Instead, they moved often from place to place. Usually they built small, temporary villages made up of large tents. They stayed in one place long enough for their horses and other livestock to rest and graze. Then they packed up their belongings and moved on.

These Asian nomads took advantage of every opportunity that came along. One opportunity came during harvest season for the farmers of the river valleys. Many farms stored a lot of grain and other foodstuffs. The nomads often raided the storehouses. They rode in on their fast horses and seemed to come out of nowhere. They stole food and livestock. They also sometimes raided villages and towns.

A Steppe Nomad's House

The central Asian steppe nomads who threatened early China were often on the move. So their houses were portable. Still, these tent-like dwellings were very sturdy. The average one was roughly 15 feet (4.6m) across. It was made of layers of animal hide or felt stretched across a wooden frame. (Felt is made from layers of sheep's wool.) Rubbing animal fat into the hides or felt made the tent waterproof. The residents cooked on a central wood-burning hearth made of stones. The smoke escaped through a small hole cut in the ceiling.

Modern day nomads' houses in Mongolia are not that much different from those of the steppe nomads who invaded Chinese territories during the Middle Kingdom era.

The Central Military Strategy

The nomads of the steppes posed a huge challenge to the settled Chinese kingdoms. The nomads "were able to move rapidly on horseback," explains Arthur Waldron, an expert on early China. They chose "when and where to attack." Also, "by virtue of their speed," they could "concentrate superior forces against the Chinese."

Also, the Chinese rulers did not know where the invaders would strike next. The Middle Kingdom's borders were very long. There were simply not enough soldiers to guard all those borders.

The only way to keep the attackers out seemed to be to build walls. Building one across all of central Asia was out of the question. No single Chinese state could afford to do that. So each of the several kingdoms built a section of wall. These barriers could not keep all the nomads out. But a well-guarded stretch of wall *could* force a raiding party to travel many miles out of its way. That greatly slowed the enemy down.

In addition, the guards on the wall could better see the enemy coming. They could then warn people in the nearest towns or villages to be ready. Also, a ruler could order soldiers to hurry to those areas. This was the central military strategy of ancient Chinese walls, including the Great Wall.

China's early nomadic invaders were able to use their greater numbers against the Chinese at any time. In response the Chinese decided to build walls to help fend off nomadic attacks.

Those early Chinese walls were built before the **pivotal** third century BC. They no longer exist by themselves. Some decayed and fell apart over time. But most became part of a much larger fortified Great Wall. The story of this wall begins in the third century.

Chapter 2

Building the Wall's First Sections

A major turning point in ancient Chinese wall building took place after 221 BC, in the third century. The era before that date is called the Warring States Period. It was named that because the Chinese kingdoms often battled one another. Each wanted to take over the others. The main powers of the period were the Qin, Han, Zhao, Qi, Chu, Yan, and Wei.

These were the nation-states that built the earliest walls that were meant to keep invaders out. Those walls were separate. Connecting them would make a far stronger and more effective barrier. In fact, some Chinese leaders thought about combining the many walls into one or two. But it could not happen as long as China remained divided.

Unity Under the Qin

This situation changed in 221 BC. In that year Zheng, king of the Qin kingdom, finished his conquests. He had recently overcome the other warring states one by one. Now, for the first time in history, China was a single, unified empire. To celebrate his great victory, King Zheng changed his name. He became known as Qin Shihuang.

The emperor wanted to ensure that his huge new realm would last. He knew that the steppe nomads would not allow that goal. In particular, the Xiongnu tribes in the north continued to attack.

So one of Qin Shihuang's first acts as emperor was to strengthen the defensive walls. The huge project consisted of more than merely repairing them. It also required the creation of many miles of new wall sections. The work took about nine or ten years to complete. And the end product was both strong and impressive. It was also historically important. The Qin walls were the first major sections of what came to be called the Great Wall of China.

Meng Tian Takes Charge

The Qin wall stretched for more than 3,100 miles (5,000km). It was built in three major parts. The first and easternmost began in the Liaodong Peninsula, along the Yellow Sea. It ran to the west,

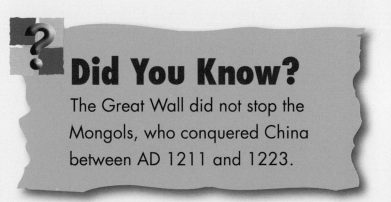

Did You Know?

The Great Wall did not stop the Mongols, who conquered China between AD 1211 and 1223.

skirting southern Mongolia, to the Yellow River. The wall's other two parts were farther west. They ended up in what is now Gansu Province in north-central China.

Building these long sections of fortified wall was very hard. This was partly because the Xiongnu and other nomadic tribes continued to invade China's borders. The emperor gave his most trusted

The Versatile Meng Tian

The Qin general who built large sections of the Great Wall had many talents. First, he was a skilled military commander. He had a major victory over the northern steppe nomads. Meng Tian was also a talented architect and builder. This is shown by his work on the Great Wall. The early Chinese also credited Meng Tian with inventing the writing brush. But modern scholars suspect this was not true. They think that tool already existed and that he merely improved it somehow.

Qin general Meng Tian, shown on this plaque on the Great Wall, defeated the nomadic invaders and took charge of building the wall.

general, Meng Tian, the task of dealing with the intruders.

Ancient writings claim that the general's army was 300,000 strong. Modern military experts say this is highly doubtful. No ancient nation was able to equip, feed, and pay that many soldiers for very long. Meng Tian's forces more likely numbered in the tens of thousands.

However big Meng Tian's army was, it defeated the Xiongnu. The emperor also gave the general another major task. It was to take charge of the wall-building project. A job that big required several key elements. The first was a large workforce. Second, thousands of animals were needed to pull wagons bearing supplies. Besides building materials, those supplies included millions of tons of food for the workers. In addition, many new roads had to be built. Otherwise, the wagons could not deliver supplies to remote areas.

The Workers

Of these diverse elements, the most important was the workforce. The exact number of people who worked on the Qin wall is unknown. Ancient and modern estimates range from a few hundred thousand to well over 1 million.

Evidence suggests that these workers were divided into three main groups. Some were soldiers. Military men who were not needed as fighters or guards did construction jobs. Also, Meng Tian's defeat of the Xiongnu freed up thousands of soldiers for work on the wall.

Criminals and slaves, as well as soldiers and peasants, worked on the Great Wall.

Many average Chinese citizens also worked on the wall. Most of them were peasant farmers. Between the planting and harvest seasons, they had a bit of free time. It was then that they joined the wall's construction crews. It is likely that doing this work paid off some or all of their annual taxes.

The third main labor force was made up of criminals. At times the government almost emptied the prisons. These workers were not paid. But their services were still not free. This was because they had to be fed and guarded, which cost money. At least some effort was made to treat the convicts fairly. One Qin law allowed some of them to go free after doing four years of hard labor.

A Warning System

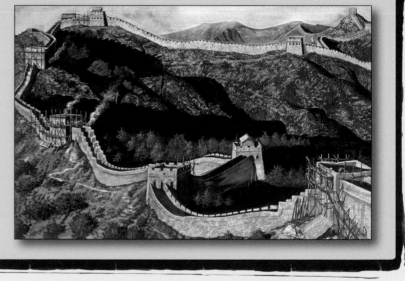

The wall had an early warning system of smoke and fire to signal the people that invaders were approaching.

The Great Wall was used for more than stopping or slowing down invaders. It was also part of a crude but effective warning system. Guards stationed on or near wall sections kept watch day and night. If they saw the enemy nearing, they sent a warning signal. In the daytime, smoke from a bonfire was used as a signal. At night the glow of the fire itself was the signal. One fire meant that about 100 intruders were coming. Two fires meant roughly 500 attackers. There were also signals for 1,000, 5,000, and 10,000 invaders.

Whether they were in chains or free, most who worked on the wall did so under very dangerous conditions. Accidents took an awful toll. Sometimes sections of old or new walls collapsed. This crushed some workers, injuring or killing them.

An unknown number of laborers also died when they fell into half-finished wall sections. Removing their bodies would have slowed down the project. So the overseers left these bodies where they were. They became entombed inside the growing monument. Such tragedies were reflected in a poem from the Qin period. "If a son is born, mind you don't raise him!" it went. "Don't you just see [that] below the Long Wall dead men's skeletons prop each other up?"

The Hangtu Method

The methods these early Chinese wall builders used were primitive by later standards. Both the Qin wall and the earlier walls it connected with were made of *hangtu*. In Chinese this means "tamped earth." Later Europeans and Americans called it rammed, or compressed, earth.

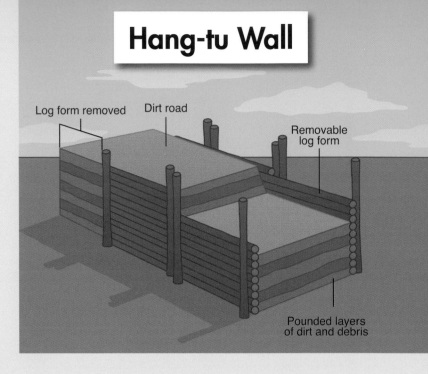

Hang-tu Wall

Log form removed   Dirt road

Removable log form

Pounded layers of dirt and debris

First, workers built a wooden framework. It looked like a long, very deep box. They poured in a layer of dirt. Next they packed it down until it was very tight and compact. Then they added a second and at times a third or fourth layer. Finally, they removed the wooden frame.

Left standing was a section of completed earthen wall.

The building materials sometimes differed from region to region. This was because various areas contained different natural materials. So at times the workers mixed gravel with dirt.

Rammed Earth Process

In the rammed earth method of wall-building, earth and gravel are poured inside removable wooden shutters (the same way concrete is poured today). Then it is tamped down one layer at a time. Each layer started out at about 7 inches (18 cm) before being compacted down to 5 inches (13 cm). These rammed-earth walls stood up particularly well in dry areas.

A section of the Qin wall in Mongolia. Most of the remaining wall has eroded and crumbled away over the centuries.

Enter the Han

More wall building took place in China in the years after Qin rule. Some rulers of the Han dynasty (202 BC to AD 220) strengthened the existing walls. Also, the emperor Han Wudi built some new sections. Wudi's additions were about 620 miles (1,000km) long. His builders used largely the same methods the Qin had.

Other times they combined twigs, marsh reeds, or other natural materials with dirt. It was vital to use local sources. To haul such heavy materials for hundreds of miles was just too time-consuming and costly.

Lifting the wood, earth, and other materials up the sides of high, steep hills was very hard. Where possible, people loaded these items into bags. They tied the bags to animals' backs. Then they drove the creatures up the hills. Another method was to use ropes to pull containers of materials upward. But just as often, workers carried the containers on their own shoulders or backs.

A few parts of the Qin walls can still be seen today. But many are gone. Some crumbled and disappeared through the effects of rain and wind. Others were replaced by bigger, stronger sections built more than 1,000 years later. These later parts of the Great Wall rose during the Ming dynasty. The wall's eventful story now turns to the work of the Ming. Without doubt, they rank among the greatest builders of all time.

Chapter 3

The Ming's Marvelous Achievement

The large defensive walls built during the Qin dynasty were historic. In a way, they marked the Great Wall's official start. Afterward, that huge structure grew larger and larger over many centuries. Many later dynasties added to this expansion.

One example was the Northern Wei dynasty (AD 386 to 534). During the reigns of its rulers, nomads continued to raid China's borders. One bothersome group of nomads were the Rouran. This tribe of people lived on the plains lying north of the Chinese. In 423 a Northern Wei ruler began work on a new wall. It was meant to halt the Rouran's attacks. This new section of the Great Wall eventually stretched for more than 600 miles (966km).

More Northern Wei wall-building projects followed. A document by a Northern Wei official named Gao Lu has survived. In 484 he urged China's leaders to add to exist-

The Northern Wei dynasty's walls were mostly built with rammed earth walls that have weathered over time.

ing sections of the Great Wall. He advised "constructing a long wall to the north." This, he claimed, would "protect against the northern barbarians." It "will require a short-term expenditure [output] of labor," he added. But "it will have permanent advantage. Once it is completed, its benefit will be for one hundred generations."

Advantages of Wall Building

In AD 484 a Northern Wei official called for building a new wall section. His name was Gao Lu. According to Arthur Waldron in his book *The Great Wall of China: From History to Myth*, Gao Lu said the new section would have several advantages. First, it "eliminates the problems of mobile defense." By this, he referred to Wei armies. They were often on the move trying to stop raids by the northern nomads. With a new defensive wall, fewer such armies would be needed. Gao also said a new section of wall "eliminates the disaster of raiding" by those nomads. And he said a new wall "removes anxiety [worry] about border defense." Finally, he said, it "permits the easy transport of supplies."

Some Northern Wei sections of the Great Wall have survived. But they are mostly in poor shape. Only archaeologists and other trained observers can appreciate their former splendor. This is because these walls were built mostly of rammed earth. Like those of the Qin, they suffered badly from weathering over time.

The same is not true of the wall sections built during the Ming dynasty (1368 to 1644). The Ming builders did not use compacted dirt. Instead, they used mostly bricks and stone. So many of the Ming defenses still retain their original size and shape. Indeed, the **zenith**, or peak, of work on the Great Wall took place under the Ming. That is why the wall's Ming-built sections are the ones most visited by modern tourists.

New, More Lethal Weapons

Every Ming ruler took part in building defensive walls. They also fixed and enlarged older wall sections. This was because nomadic tribes plagued China throughout their reigns. Among these raiders were the Tufan, Nuzhen, and Dadan.

Earlier generations of Chinese had faced similar attacks from the Asian steppes. So what made the Ming response different? Why did they switch to building with brick and stone?

The Ming builders used mostly brick and stone to construct their section of the wall from 1368 to 1644.

?

Did You Know?

The wall's highest point—at 5,033 feet (1,534 meters) above sea level—is in the Chinese capital city of Beijing.

One big reason was military in nature. In the Ming era, new, more deadly kinds of weapons were developed. Before, soldiers had used clubs, bows, swords, and spears. Thick earthen walls could easily protect against such weapons.

But partway through the Ming era, gunpowder began to be used in warfare. Cannons and handheld firearms caused far more damage than did bows and swords. These new devices made many old-style defenses **obsolete**, or outdated. That included the aging defensive walls in China. Thus, the Ming felt they had no choice but to build their walls with brick and stone.

Building with Bricks

The hardness of these materials was not the only thing that made the walls stronger. The thickness of the walls was also a factor. When bricks were used, a wall's outer facing was often seven or eight layers thick. The space inside the outer layers was filled with heavy rubble. This included huge amounts of rocks, dirt, and other debris.

Counting the brick layers and rubble, many stretches of Ming wall are 20 feet (6m) thick. Some are an amazing 40 feet (12m) thick! Their heights range from 20 feet up to 50 feet (15m). The tallest sections are as tall as a five-story office building. Firearms were no match against such huge masses of material. Millions of bricks were required for even a short stretch of Ming wall. To make them, workers gathered large amounts of clay, sand, and straw. They added some water. Then they used their feet to stomp the mixture into a dough-like material. They used this to make individual, still-moist

The Ming wall was 20 feet (6m) to 40 feet (12m) thick and from 20 to 50 feet (15m) high. It had many layered stone walls filled with heavy rubble in between the facings.

Windlasses for Lifting

Many of the large, heavy stone blocks used by the Ming builders were lifted using large but simple windlasses. In the middle of a windlass is a cylinder, or drum-shaped section. It lies horizontally, or on its side. A crank sticking out of one end of the cylinder allows people to turn it. When they do, they pull on a rope or cable wound around the cylinder. The end of the rope or cable is attached to the object to be moved. Thus, turning the crank moves the object.

The stone blocks needed for the Ming walls and towers had to be quarried, transported, lifted, and put in place with systems of ropes, pulleys, and windlasses.

bricks. Finally, they baked the bricks in hot **kilns**. A typical finished brick weighed around 22 pounds (10kg).

The builders set up hundreds of kilns near each worksite. That way the bricks did not have to be hauled for long distances. This saved a great deal of time, effort, and money. In 2002 Chinese excavators found the remains of 48 brick kilns. They were buried near a section of Ming wall. Nature had covered the kilns. Half of them still had bricks in them!

Working with Stone

Sometimes the builders mixed stacks of granite or other hard stone between layers of brick. In others cases they built a stretch of wall solely with stone. Also, they built many stone watchtowers and beacon towers. From the watchtowers, soldiers kept an eye out for invaders. The beacon towers were used for making fires to send warning signals. The exact number of towers the Ming built is not known. But modern experts agree it was in the tens of thousands.

The stone blocks needed to build the Ming walls and towers had to be hewn, or cut, from **quarries**. To do this, workers used iron hammers and chisels. Whenever possible, the quarries were located near the worksites. This was because the stones were very heavy. And moving them was very hard and time-consuming. Many of the stones are 6.5 feet (2m) wide and weigh 1 ton (0.9t) or more.

Workers moved these heavy blocks using systems of ropes and pulleys. Lifting devices called windlasses were also used. Still another method was to build a large earthen ramp beside a section of wall. Animals dragged stones up the ramp. Workers then put them in place atop the wall. When that section was finished, they tore down the ramp and moved on.

Proud of Their Achievement

Sometimes the Ming builders did not erect new walls from scratch. Instead, they chose older wall sections seen as useful. These earlier walls were made of rammed earth. The Ming builders first repaired them if necessary. Then they made those sections the bases of newer walls. They added layers of bricks atop the restored earthen walls. Where needed, they built brick or stone watchtowers beside them.

On the Great Wall many reliefs, carvings, and writings describe building methods, and include the names of dignitaries, workers, and historical events.

The Leftover Brick

A number of colorful stories have survived from the Ming period of wall building. One was the story of a worker named Yi Kaizhan. He was very skilled at math. When the builders reached the Jiayuguan Pass, he approached his supervisor. It would take a certain number of bricks to build this section of wall, Yi Kaizhan said. The supervisor was a cruel man. He said that this estimate had better be right. If it was off by even a single brick, every worker would be punished. After three years, the project was completed. Sure enough, a single leftover brick was lying on the ground. The supervisor prepared to punish the workers. But Yi Kaizhan warned against it. A god had put the brick there, he said. If anyone touched the object, the entire wall would collapse. The fearful supervisor did not want to take a chance. So he left the brick where it was. Some people say it is still there today.

One way that modern experts learn about these walls is by looking at them closely. This tells them which building methods were used in certain time periods. They also look at ancient writings about the Great Wall. Some of these are carved or painted on the wall's bricks and stones. Often they list the supervisors and others who built a specific wall section. One example from 1576 says: "Ensign Sun Erh-Kuo, Superintendent of Works, Lui Ching, Military Contractor, and others to the number of 130 names

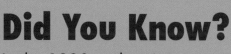

Did You Know?

In the 1930s, when Japan invaded China, some Chinese used parts of the Great Wall for defense.

cooperated in building this extension of 591 feet [of wall]. . . . The completion of the construction was reported . . . on the 16th day of the 9th moon of the 4th year of Wan Li."

One cannot blame those who built the Great Wall for being proud of their achievement. In the closing years of the Ming era, it was a true wonder of the world. But most of the world still knew nothing about it. For countless centuries, only the people of central and eastern Asia had seen the wall. However, that situation was about to change.

Chapter 4

The Wall's Lofty Living Legacy

When the Ming additions to the Great Wall were complete, it was truly immense. No one knows for sure how much earth, stone, and brick it held. One modern estimate says it equaled the sum of all the buildings that were in Britain in the 1790s. Another claims the wall's materials could create 120 mounds the size of Egypt's largest pyramid.

A Distant Wonder

Such a huge structure was bound to attract attention. But during the Ming period, few people outside China knew it existed. The Ming period ended in 1644. But China was still largely isolated from the rest of the world. Outsiders knew of the wall mainly through rumors. A handful of long-distance traders and missionaries made the long journey from Europe

Italian mapmaker Martino Martini made this crude map of China in the early 1700s.

to China. They claimed to have seen a huge wall. They said this wall stretched to the horizon.

Among these early travelers was Matteo Ricci. He was an Italian Catholic priest. Ricci lived for a while in China. Before his death in 1610, he kept a diary. It was first published in Europe in 1615. The diary mentions the Great Wall. "To the north," it says, "the country is defended against hostile [intruders] by [an] unbroken line of defense." It includes "a tremendous wall four hundred and five miles long."

The wall was much longer than Ricci's estimate. Still, his diary sparked interest in the wall among Europeans. So did the work of an Italian mapmaker a century later. Martino Martini made a crude map of China. It was based on reports by traders and other travelers. His map showed a long wall. The wall made up China's northern border. That huge structure, he wrote, was built "215 years before Christ." It was "magnificent, huge, and admirable," he stated.

Martini never saw the wall himself. But an Englishman named George Macartney did. In 1793 He visited China's

Exploding a Great Wall Myth

Many myths have been told about the Great Wall over the years. One well-known myth involves the moon. It claims the wall is visible from that heavenly body. The idea came from a 1925 *National Geographic* article quoted in the website about the wall, *The Great Wall of China and the Grand Canal.* "According to astronomers," it began, only one "work of man's hands" is "visible from the moon." That work "is the Great Wall of China." In reality, though, the claim is false. The wall can be seen by astronauts orbiting fairly close to Earth. But even that happens only when lighting conditions arc just right. The moon is many times farther away. Seeing the wall from there would be like seeing a human hair from 2 miles (3.2km) away.

capital, Beijing. On the way, he visited the wall. He was overwhelmed by the sight of it. He later said, "It is certainly the most stupendous work of human hands. For I imagine that if the outline of all the masonry [stone] of all the forts and fortified places in the whole world were to be calculated, it would fall considerably short of that of the Great Wall of China."

From Neglect to National Pride

More foreign accounts of the Great Wall were written in the two centuries that followed. They made it clear that the structure was largely abandoned in the 1600s. Chinese leaders did not feel it was needed. So they ignored it and no longer kept it up. This neglect continued decade after

Did You Know?

In 2008, well-known singers from around the world took part in a large rock concert on the wall.

Chinese Communist soldiers march along the Great Wall. Some sections of the wall were destroyed in fighting in 1949.

decade. It became even worse under the **Communist** Chinese. They seized power in 1949. Some sections of the wall were destroyed during China's early Communist period.

China is still under Communist rule. But its leaders have let it become more open to the outside world. Each year the Chinese welcome millions of visitors to their country. They proudly show off their cultural heritage. It includes much fine art and literature from past ages.

The wall was ignored for many years. But that finally began to change in 1976. In that year Deng Xiaoping became China's new leader. He wanted to preserve the country's cultural heritage. That included the Great Wall. "Let us love our country and restore our Great Wall," he

In 1976 China's new leader, Deng Xiaoping, adopted a policy of preserving the country's cultural heritage and restoring huge sections of the wall through the 1980s.

said. In the 1980s major repairs began on many sections of the wall.

Many modern Chinese take special pride in the Great Wall. They feel that in a way it speaks to the rest of the world. It shows what their ancestors were capable of. And it stands for Chinese civilization's many great feats. For these reasons, the wall has become their national symbol.

A Striking Structure

The wall is also, by far, China's number one tourist attraction. Most people who visit the wall today go to Badaling. It is situated about 43 miles (69km) north of Beijing. The segment of wall there is called the Badaling Great Wall. It was built by the Ming. It is made almost entirely of brick and stone. Its stout

Causes of Damage to the Wall

Several factors have contributed to the damage the Great Wall has suffered over the years. First, wind and rain have steadily eaten away at it. Also, shifting desert sands have buried some sections. Modern wars have taken a heavy toll, too. Often, soldiers hid behind parts of the walls. That invited enemy aircraft, tanks, and bombs to batter the wall. Damage was also done by poor peasants living near the wall. They took bricks and stones from it to build new houses. Sometimes government officials were to blame. In a thoughtless manner, they tore down wall sections to make way for new roads.

Most people who visit the wall today go to Badaling. It is the best preserved of the wall's surviving sections.

defenses, walkways, and towers are grandly and beautifully built. In a spectacular way, they wind through a set of low, rugged hills. This striking structure is the best-preserved of the wall's surviving sections.

In 1987 the Great Wall got a fabulous honor. It was included in the World Cultural Heritage Directory. This is put out by the United Nations. The directory lists the world's most superb creations.

Another major honor for the Great Wall came in 2007. That year, it became one of the New Seven Wonders of the World. Among the others is the dazzling Taj Mahal tomb in India. The grand lost city of Macchu Picchu in Peru is also one of the seven. (The Great Wall was not one of the Seven Ancient Wonders, which were chosen in the late second century BC. This is because they were chosen by a Greek,

Antipater of Sidon. For him China was a faraway, mostly legendary land. He was not even aware the wall existed.)

Preserving the Wall

Everyone who visits the Badaling Great Wall is impressed. But that memorable experience can be misleading. Some visitors think the wall's other sections are equally grand. But the sad truth is that many of them are in bad shape. Some are actually crumbling back into the earth.

Saving the wall's remaining sections has become a major priority in China. In 2006 the government passed laws to pro-

Visitors make their way along a restored section of the wall. Saving the wall's remaining sections has become a top priority of the Chinese government.

Taking the New Laws Seriously

Most Chinese see the Great Wall as a precious piece of their heritage. So they are committed to saving it. The proof of this is how seriously they take the new laws passed to protect it. In 2008 five men were arrested. They had been caught digging for iron ore very near the wall. Most residents of the region were appalled. They agreed with the court that sentenced the men to three years in prison.

tect them. One made it illegal to remove bricks from the wall. Another banned carving messages into it. Also banned is digging in the ground within 656 feet (200m) of the wall.

All across China, people hope these laws will help. They are glad for the on-going efforts to restore the wall. They view it much as Americans see the Statue of Liberty. So they want to see a bright future for China's national symbol. As Chinese newspaper reporter Zhang Zhi-hua put it, "Loving and repairing the Great Wall" shows "the patriotic feelings of the Chinese people."

These feelings were put into words by a Chinese writer named Cheng Dalin. In 1984 he wrote a book about the Great Wall. In it, he called the wall "the most awesome structure ever devised by man." In his view, Chinese civilization gave the world one of its finest gifts. For the many Chinese who would agree with him, that is the wall's lofty living **legacy**.

Glossary

archaeologists [ark-eh-ALL-a-jistz]: Scientists who dig up and study lost civilizations.

Chang Cheng [SHANG-Shing]: "Great Wall" in ancient Chinese.

Communist [COM-you-nist]: A follower of a political, economic, and social system in which the government owns and runs the factories and other sources of wealth and the people share money and goods equally. China became a Communist nation in 1949.

excavators [EX-ka-vay-turz]: People who dig up objects from the ground.

hangtu [hahng-TOO]: "Tamped earth" in ancient Chinese; dirt that has been highly compressed into a hard mass.

kilns [kilnz]: Small ovens used for drying pottery objects or bricks.

legacy [LEG-a-see]: Something one person or group inherits from another.

missionary [MISH-un-air-ee]: Someone who goes to foreign lands to teach them about his or her religious beliefs.

nomads [NO-madz]: People who move from place to place rather than living permanently in the same place.

obsolete [ob-so-LEET]: Outdated or no longer useful.

pivotal [PIV-uh-tl]: Very important.

quarries [KWAR-eez]: Rocky places from which people cut and remove slabs of stone.

steppes [stepz]: Grass-covered plains.

zenith [ZEE-nith]: The peak or highest point.

For More Information

Books

Terry Collins, *Ancient China: An Interactive History Adventure.* Mankato, MN: Capstone, 2012.

Robert Coupe, *The Great Wall of China.* New York: Powerkids, 2013.

Muriel L. Dubois, *Ancient China: Beyond the Great Wall.* Mankato, MN: Capstone, 2011.

Cynthia Henzel, *The Great Wall of China.* Edina, MN: Checkerboard, 2011.

Natalie M. Rosinsky, *Ancient China.* Mankato, MN: Compass Point, 2012.

Websites

Chinese History for Beginners, Condensed China
http://condensedchina.com

Chrystalinks, Great Wall of China
www.crystalinks.com/greatwallofchina.html

Travel China Guide, Great Wall Sections
www.travelchinaguide.com/china_great_wall/scene/

UNESCO World Heritage List, Great Wall
http://whc.unesco.org/en/list/438

Index

About the Author

Historian and award-winning writer Don Nardo has published numerous books for young people about the ancient world. They cover the histories, cultures, religions, myths, and daily lives of the Babylonians, Egyptians, Greeks, Romans, and other peoples of the distant past.